Anywho, I Love You

Samantha King Holmes | r.h. Sin | Graham Holmes

Andrews McMeel
PUBLISHING®

Sin's Introduction

Falling in love after you've had your heart destroyed by someone you believed loved you makes it increasingly difficult to trust again. You meet a person, you develop feelings for them, and you're once again faced with this decision of putting the foundation of your future into new hands, hoping that it all turns out the way you imagined.

I think it's important to remember that even while you may find heartache familiar and even though you've been hurt several times before, that person in front of you is not the person who hurt you. It takes a wild type of courage to love again when everything you've loved has turned to dust, but you mustn't allow the past to take hold and dictate your future.

This was something I learned over time; there are lessons in heartache and, even though it hurts, pain can be a stairway to something better. You just have to utilize the experience of betrayal to identify the red flags and warning signs. Think about it for a second; you are heavily experienced in the realm of mistreatment and distrust and so you know exactly what to look for when looking for the person to spend your life with.

Love doesn't come easy; for some of us, we'll find that we have to fall for the wrong people just to figure out what is right. The love you deserve, the romance you long for, is often hidden behind all those people who intend to waste your time, and so that means you must navigate through halls of heartbreak in order to discover a version of love that will encourage you to feel whole.

That pathway to love also begins with self. The way you treat yourself is a template for the way others are to treat you. Practicing self-love will save you the trouble of settling in relationships that distract you from cultivating love and a peace of mind. Self-love is also the cure after the breakup, the elixir that will keep you sane in preparation for new experiences and adventures on the path leading to your soul mate.

Most relationships are lessons on what isn't love, and it's only after you're done hurting that you come to a realization that the person who broke your heart was never worthy of an emotional reaction. The suffering is not love; waking up each day struggling to get out of bed, fighting to keep your eyes open is not love. Those moments when you're made to feel like your sadness or pain is an inconvenience are not love. The hours you go on, fighting to get through the day while dealing with bouts of loneliness even as that person sits beside you aren't love. The days when you think of leaving and staying feels like settling are not love.

So often you stay only because you fear you're losing something, but that person who forces you to deal with their emotional absence or lack of effort is not a loss. That individual who makes you feel guilty for feeling anything at all is not a loss. Your partner who seems to be playing on the opposite team and or refuses to cooperate in a way that promotes peacefulness and progression is not a loss.

Relationships worthy of your energy do not pose the type of difficulty that keeps happiness and tranquility at a distance. A relationship worthy of your devotion will not stand in the way of self-love and healing. There were moments in my own life when the person I was with became a distraction, a roadblock between myself and the path I knew I should take, and it's only after you get through that roadblock that you find yourself closer to a love that actually feels true.

Real love is rare; it's not easy to find because it doesn't sit on the surface. It is embedded deep, away from eyes, only to be felt, an experience like no other. And as hard as it may be, you will have to surpass all the people standing in the way of everything you deserve. Each breakup, each heartbreak, and several people you believed you loved will need to be left behind for the sake of discovering someone worthy of all that you have to offer.

In my own life, I learned to grasp the concept of moving on and the rewards in letting go. It didn't come easy. My war-torn heart has seen many battles and, I'll be honest, at times I've felt I'd lost. But as time would teach me, most of the people you meet will not be capable of providing whatever you need that will encourage your heart to keep beating for them and, at some point, you're going to have to learn that your heart is always yours, no matter how often you've given it away.

You will eventually return to yourself; you will somehow find a way back home. And when you get there, you'll have a wealth of knowledge about what to avoid going further. The biggest lessons in love come from the people who aren't brave enough to be honest with your heart. And those lessons can be utilized as stepping-stones across the waters of true love.

Despite the betrayal.

It's beautiful, the way you're able to love as if you've never been hurt. It takes a lot of courage to move forward after heartache and still pursue the love you believe you deserve. And while it hasn't happened yet, I hope you know that every ending brings you closer to your destination. Every lie will make the truth so much sweeter, and the triumph of finding someone who will care for your heart and match your effort will be so much more rewarding due to all you've already been through.

There are some of you reading this right now who are close to giving up, and I want you to know that you can't let your past dictate your future. Don't give power to people who no longer deserve an emotional reaction from you. You can't let your exes prevent you from realizing that there is something better out there for you.

There's this feeling of hopelessness in the air whenever true love gets brought up. There's despair and indifference. Too often, we allow the wrong people into our lives, and they leave us with a bit less hope in the idea of finding a soul mate. It's challenging to continue to go after the one thing you've been denied. It's hard to continue the pursuit of something that doesn't seem to exist. Real love is a hard sell to anyone who has had their heart broken a couple of times. And despite your reason for losing belief, I think you mustn't ever allow the past to tell your future's story.

Alone with stars.

the emptiness always feels
the heaviest after midnight

the moon melancholy
sitting alone searching for stars

two lovers lost beneath the same sky
longing to be in each other's arms

restless nights
when dreams are misplaced
with eyes closed tight
attempting to imagine that stranger's face

you didn't hear me
my voice muffled
beneath all the things
you were distracted by

you rarely saw me
your sight pulled away
by screens

my absence
will be soft at first
but with time
you will feel like
the air is thinning

and when you finally
lift yourself to search for me
my ghost will haunt
the corners of your heart

r.h. Sin

Internal talk 1.

I think real love looks different for everyone, but at the core of any loving relationship is kindness, patience, transparency, and devotion. Too often the heart falls for someone who isn't prepared to care for it because many of us love in an attempt to feel a void rather than to add to what joy and peace we've already cultivated. Sure enough, a person can enter your life and change it in a way that makes you feel whole, but giving this type of power to someone who turns out to be the wrong person can leave you depleted to the point in which your idea of love is altered in a negative way.

Love yourself before you search for love in someone else. A lesson I needed to learn in my own life.

Anywho, I Love You

loving the wrong person
is like trying to live
without a pulse

Internal talk 2.

they tell you to search for a spark
the only problem with that
is sparks are usually anticlimactic
moments that have no longevity

Internal talk 3.

i'm fine with a candle that burns continuously
or, even better, a volcano that remains on fire
from within for several lifetimes

Internal talk 4.

Sometimes you have to break up with your family so that you can create the type of family you always wanted.

There's always this fear accompanied by an impending sense of regret. It's scary to think that you will lose the ones who know you best, but then again, there is this need to detach from the people who have forced you to lose yourself beneath the weight of their neglect, lack of appreciation, and constant judgment. I found more of me, the parts I'd hidden just to satisfy the ones who should have loved me unconditionally. Swept under beds and rugs, made a secret to those who had no intention of ever respecting my feelings and ideas. Who knew my freedom would live in their absence? So much joy kept from me for the sake of staying connected, only to figure out that the happiness I'd been searching for resided in the opposite direction of the people I thought I needed.

Anywho, I Love You

self-love is like a lighthouse
your soul mate will see
the light you project

A droplet.

i fall for and fall with the rain
i move through the air carelessly
in search of somewhere to land
in need of someone to touch
a desire to be caught and felt

a gentle storm of water
carried with the wind
in search of you

To those with hope.

Never run from the truth of what you're feeling. You must always face your harshest and most painful emotions. You will never heal until you truly see yourself and the pain that lives within your heart. You will never heal until you've identified the source of that sadness. The longer you run from your emotional truths, the harder it will be to leave behind the people and things that break your heart. It won't be easy, but the only way to begin the process of healing is to be honest with yourself, no pretending to be okay. And no more making excuses to be with someone who doesn't deserve you.

There's this overwhelming desire for something new, something better, living within your heart. You want to break free; you just don't know where to start. But I'm hoping that, with time, you'll figure out that, within yourself, you have everything you need and more. I hope you realize that you have more than enough on your own, and maybe that'll make it easier for you to leave behind the things that don't deserve a space in your life.

Night of courage.

the moon just sat there
draped in darkness
unafraid of all the things
that live in the night
and i thought to myself
"i want to be that brave"

Internal talk 5.

It's a beautiful thing to have legs that will run to put distance between yourself and those who hurt you. It is a blessing to have a heart that will love again when the moment is right.

Choice in direction.

what if what you pictured
doesn't fill the frame
and instead of igniting it
that something weakens the flame

what if the truth was just a lie
covered in beautiful bows
and instead of urging you to stay
it inspired you to go

what if where you are
was never the place you should be
what if loving yourself despite the heartache
is the way toward setting you free

what if what comes later
is the future that will stick
if you go back to who hurt you
something better is what you'll miss

what if . . .

the idea of you
inspired God
to make woman

<u>Someone needs this.</u>

i know it's hard to believe
but i hope you find someone
who helps you fall in love
without caution or safety nets

a love you can be certain about
with someone who is sure about
the way they feel for you

<u>Serendipity.</u>

traveling miles to a strange city
to meet a girl i've only known
through a screen
because she has silenced
the noises in my head
and i need to know
exactly what this means

Goodbye, Tampa.

years, we spent years together
and nothing worked
i was cold during your summers
and your winters were never enough

i outgrew you long ago
it was over but i stayed

thank you for letting me walk away
i found home the moment i left you
and things will never be the same

Don't it feel like you're searching for something that doesn't exist? It is a love that doesn't break, a feeling everlasting with someone consistently ready to do whatever it takes to remind your heart that it is loved. Why do the kindest hearts go through so much pain? Rain falls mainly for those who deserve the sun. It almost feels hopeless to keep hoping for something you've never known. Tired of settling, tired of heartache, weary from constantly having to let go.

I feel you; I see you. I hear you, wishing for a life of love upon dead stars. Fighting for the wrong person from the belief that, if you try harder, they'll finally understand that you are worthy of their devotion, but love doesn't work that way. You can't keep investing your energy into someone who refuses to acknowledge and or respect that effort.

The road toward the love you deserve will be paved with misfortune and undeserving people with their hands out, urging you to fall with no intention to catch you. I just hope you decide to move forward; I just hope you refuse to stay where you are not appreciated.

Eventually, you have to stop expecting something true from people who have always decided to lie to you. There is no truth to be found in pursuing any relationship with someone fraudulent. I know it's not easy; I'm not implying that letting go will be easy, but you mustn't allow yourself to stay in a relationship that keeps you from the love you know you deserve.

Free falling.

love is a waltz to a heavy metal melody
like walking beneath snowstorms
cultivating and maintaining peace
in a moment of chaos

you see fire, but you're unafraid
aware of the risk, but you keep moving
calm in the midst of turbulence
hand in hand with the one
who will keep you safe

you're never lost when beside your beloved
strange lands become adventures
destinations made unimportant
for you have already arrived
when in love

i know this
because i found it in her
nestled in the frame
of her warm brown eyes
protected from the chill of winter
a cool breeze as she whispers my name
in the months of summer

i love her

Internal talk 6.

I wanted her to know that she didn't have to fuck me for the sake of holding my attention. There was no pressure, no need for an incentive. All I really wanted was the opportunity to know what moved her, what made her happy. I wanted to know what I could add to her life and if she'd be willing to give me the chance to discover the magic that others had overlooked.

She's more than just a body. She holds the key to the future, maybe mine.

Anywho, I Love You

we were strangers
but i'm sure
i'd recognized you
for the millionth time

Time travel.

suppose i could go back
to visit me at a younger age
that hopeless kid standing
out front on the edge of a cliff
carved out by disappointment and pain

i'd tap myself on the shoulder to say, "hold on
be patient, because what waits for you in the future
will overshadow and overpower all the demons
that are chasing you right now"

Remind myself.

if you see courage
inside her heart
acknowledge it
if you hear meaning
in her words
always listen
if she loves you
like nothing before
honor her devotion
by loving her
like nothing else matters

Twin souls.

i don't love you
because you're perfect
i love you because
when you're not around
it's as if my soul
has left my body

Anywho, I Love You

grateful for all the endings
that helped me begin with you

r.h. Sin

i just hope you forgive me
for taking so long
to love you

8:22am, New Rochelle.

the beautiful perfume
of a blossoming rose

your scent lingers here
even when your body
isn't present

your touch etched
into my skin
like a tattoo

you move through me
like reason
you spark my imagination
like ideas

and you set my soul free
from the bondage of heartache

you are the very thing
that leaped out of my dreams
so that in the here and now
love can reign over my life

she wasn't lost
she wandered
in the direction
of self-love

You always knew me.

soul mates know things
about one another
before they ever meet

you were the stranger
with all of my secrets

This journey forward.

I walked through the broken shards of my own heart barefoot in hopes of finding someone who could muster up the strength to love me the way I needed. Broken and afraid, I found the courage to walk into darkness not knowing what I would find on the other side. I burned bridges that led to nowhere, took exits away from the familiar. All so that I can be closer to something worth fighting for.

The journey toward a relationship worthy of your emotional energy is filled with disappointment and lies. And everything you want more than anything can seem so far away.

it was raining that afternoon
i think the sun was crying

Naturally.

perhaps the ones
who came before you
were just reminders
that there was something better
out there for me

so often i tried to force them
to be the one
and walked away with nothing
until i ran into you

After you heal.

There's a moment in time when the heartache becomes relief. That present ordeal of pain becomes easier to leave behind you. It may not feel like it in the moment, but the best is yet to come. Someone you haven't met will be better than what you've had. And the joy you cultivate will overshadow all that fucking heartbreak.

It was never about the way she looked, and even though she's the most beautiful presence in my life, the extent of what keeps me falling in love with her every day goes much deeper than skin. It was never about what I could get from her, and as much as I long for the moments when I could be cradled inside her essence, my love for her began way before we were ever physical. I was more concerned about the person she was within, and since the day we began to communicate, I was more focused on what I could provide as a potential mate and how much I could devote in effort to show her how much I care. See, they want you to believe that you must compromise yourself to get someone to like you. They want you to believe that getting a man's attention is more important than knowing what it feels like to be with someone who simply wants you because they deserve you and who wants to prove that they deserve you, who'd do any and everything to fight for the opportunity to be with you. For me, no one can take the place of this woman in this photo because I wouldn't dare give anyone else the chance. Unbreakable bonds are created upon the foundation of respect and loyalty. Love is founded on the grounds of communication, devotion, respect, and loyalty. I'm devoted to this woman, not for what she looks like but more for what she represents. I'm devoted to this woman because she chose to allow me into her life and doing something like that is a form of courage. I'm devoted to this woman, my wife, because my heart found its soul mate the moment I heard her laugh. True love dwells much deeper than the surface; real love can only reside in the core of whoever is brave enough to feel it and provide it. Samantha, thank you for changing my life.

Meeting.

the first time i met you
it felt nostalgic

strangers, yet familiar
soul mates beginning
a friendship

a like that would easily
become love

where winters once thrived
my heart is now an endless summer
my soul a garden where roses now bloom

you're a dream
but i'm awake
a calm
in the center of storms

a stillness
in raging water
a light
in the breath of midnight

holding you is like coming home
a kiss from you
is like a walk through Rome

r.h. Sin

Manhattan, my love.

what the city doesn't scream, it whispers
the wind a stale cold, the sky a dark gray
a storm isn't just arriving, it's coming home

for the rain clouds with droplets
that turn to snow
have always found a place to rest
on these city streets

amid the chaos, peace lives
if you stare into the abyss long enough
there's hope among the hopeless

there is a past, a present, and future
my life, a rose that grows
in the concrete jungle

Anywho, I Love You

the trouble will always be with timing
for i am afraid that forever
will never be long enough
and i will always have hope
to meet you sooner
so that i could love you longer

she is deep water
a woman with depth
she flows into my life
bringing love with her waves
and inspiration to my shores

Paris, fall.

Paris, a burnt rust
leaves abandoning trees
escaping to the surface
lying beneath my wife's feet

i finally know what love is
i've seen her face
looking back at me
while i hold this camera

she's standing against the wind
like a monument erected
in the name of strength and beauty

my Queen
a beret is her crown
the Luxembourg Garden
her kingdom

<u>Dear Samantha.</u>

Since the moment we first spoke, I imagined an entire life with you. The moment I heard you laugh, I knew my heart would be yours forever. I've spent the majority of my life in search of a greater purpose, and I found something and someone to finally be passionate about the moment we began to build our friendship and relationship. The last four years have been everything I knew they could be and more. You have consistently been the most precious thing in my life. You are my world, and with you here by my side, I always know that I can do any and everything. You are the song my heart sings in the morning, and you are still the greatest dream I have whenever I close my eyes at night. You are the most powerful woman I know and the most inspiring person I've ever met. You intrigue me, you excite me, and your love is the whisper that calms the sea in my soul. Thank you for being such an amazing wife and friend. Thank you for choosing me, and thank you for devoting yourself to this marriage.

The child inside your womb . . . our son . . . will one day soon know the love that you've brought into my life. Our baby will one day know what it means to be wrapped in the arms of a Queen. Our son, your son, our baby will be the luckiest child on this planet to have known the love that exists within your heart. Thank you for carrying him. Thank you for protecting him. Thank you for loving him, and thank you for loving me. Happy New Year, from your loving husband, the father of your child, your best friend. I love you.

So often the lessons in love are presented to us by people who have no intention of loving us in the way we desire or the way they promised.

When I look into your eyes, I see and hear the truth, even before you speak it. Your promises are more than words; they arrive bundled in action and devotion. This love, our love, built on a solid foundation because of the time and energy we've invested into one another. Your lessons in love, the one you're presenting to me right now, overshadows all the things I was taught before you. Your version of love keeps me free from the bondage of the past and the chains of sadness.

Anywho, I Love You

i've been in your arms so long
that you are the only thing
my body remembers

touched by you so many times
that your fingers and hands
can tell the story of my life
without words

My Son.

i find solace in those deep-brown eyes
the child in me awakened by your energy
i'd waited so long for you, Graham
traveling miles through life's anguish
just so that i could reach you
learning as much as i can
just so that i could teach you

but you teach me

heartfelt lessons in your kisses
a story of true love
in your embrace

i'd constructed this picture
of how it would be
once we met
but here in this moment
you've exceeded
any expectation i could have

thank you for choosing me
when you did
my inspiration to keep going
my inspiration to live

and all this time, i believed my writing
was the most beautiful thing
i'd created, until i held my son
for the first time

Ellie.

daughter, my love
you stare at me
flaws and all
but to you
i'm perfect

your eyes lit like two moons
your smile could raise the sun
you are a complete vision of joy
you are heaven in my arms

you hold me in your tiny hands
my finger in your grasp
your lips widen for a smile
your eyes slightly closed
to express an overwhelming joy

you don't even know what happiness is
not old enough to understand the language
but you are the author of my joy
i am holding a representation of bliss
with you in my embrace

you are an inspiration, salvation from the chaos
you are joyfulness in a world burdened by anguish
you are my guiding light
toward happiness
whenever i forget to smile

Strength and love.

twice, i bared witness
a touch of agony on your face
torn inside out
in effort to bring forth fruit

you've blessed my life
in abundance
you've shared your body
not only with me
but also with our little loves

together, we've manifested
two beautiful dreams
but you alone embodying the strength
to help them enter this world

and i thank you for that . . .

my son keeps me curious
the way he looks into the morning sky
i keep searching for what he sees
i long to feel the way he feels
witnessing the sunrise
kissing the Empire State Building
on its way up

Year 2022.

you're a wild dream
a reason to remain asleep
they should build skyscrapers
and name them after you

if you were metal
you'd be something
out of this world
crashed into Earth
discovered only by digging deep

your existence is legendary
and each day you walk this Earth
history is made

your voice is both
a sweet symphony and battle cry
nothing but anthems
come forth from your lips

you are a woman
a majestic being
you are my wife
my truest love

r.h. Sin

There will come a moment when my past will become a picture show, moving quickly through all the scenes that have made up my life, and I know, even now, that every strip of film containing you will be my favorite to watch.

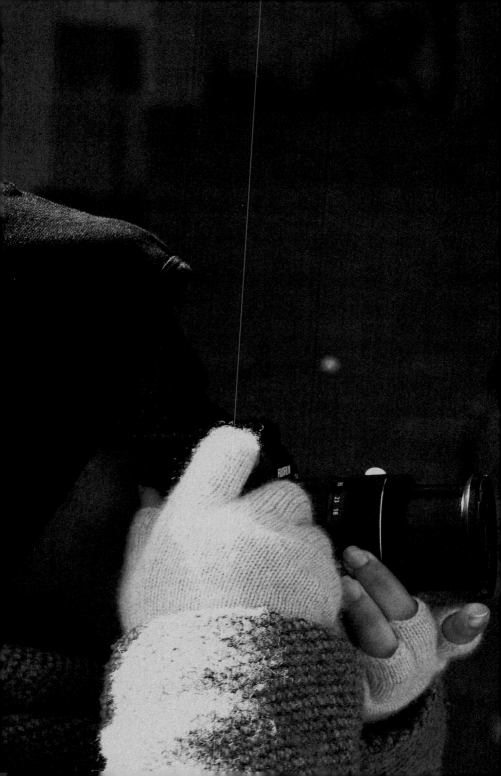

r.h. Sin

There really isn't anything like you because there was nothing before you. My rain-soaked days and cloudiest of gray skies found color the moment you drifted into my life. A somber song transformed into a beautiful melody. And this feeling of nostalgia for a person I'd never known was both confusing and delightful. We didn't meet like strangers; the first time was like the last time that didn't even exist, well at least in this lifetime. The way water flows back into itself is the way I moved in your direction. Without question, you are the answer. Without a doubt, you are hope, a beautiful idea, a profound statement, presented in a form that I could touch, hold, and love.

I knew since the very first day that I would do anything to live out my life beside you.

Anywho, I Love You

i had a dream last night
the sky was on fire
the ground beneath me
soft as putty

i witnessed skyscrapers
begin to sink
as if their foundations
were quicksand

precipitation filled the air
rain carried by the wind
tornadoes formed offshore
in preparation to meet land

waves reaching toward the heavens
tsunamis were literally
being born

and Earth caught fire
as volcanic mountains erupted

i stood there in disbelief
because as the world turned
and rushed toward a dreadful end
there were no feelings of fear within me

what i felt was gratitude
for i spent the remainder
of my days
tucked away in the embrace
of the people i've loved the most

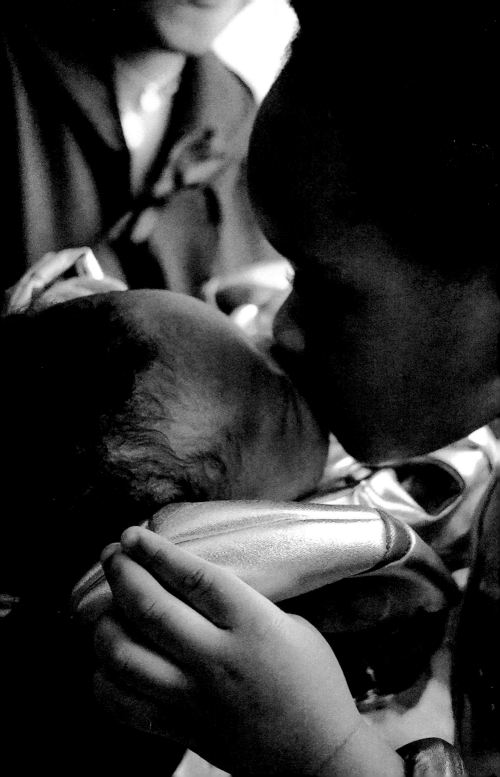

Graham Holmes

Graham Holmes

Samantha King Holmes

We allow people to plant seeds of doubt within us
even after someone is no longer in our lives
We don't stop to root out all the negativity we
  allowed to grow
We just let it poison our perspective of self
without realizing that sometimes our words
  aren't our own
They're just something someone said once
that we allowed ourselves to believe and
  make our truth

Touch the sky

Before I was seven
she bound my wings
with her fears and lies
told me I couldn't fly
that I was safer on the ground

My wings grew stronger
so, she broke them
held my hand
and told me this was my place

So, I expanded my mind
flew around inside
where she couldn't see it
kept my dreams a secret

She fed me nothing but her doubts
skewed perceptions of reality
I didn't realize that she needed me this way
Agonized at the thought of me
soaring above her

I found one day
she had left me
wounded, easy prey
I learned to fight, survive
despite the hardships
I did not miss her

Life took a knife
shoved it in and twisted for good measure
Now I walk with slumped shoulders, head bowed
as if life deserves me humbled
I miss the days I believed in myself
and thought nothing was impossible

My wings healed
I have touched the sky
Glided on the wind
Something always pulls me back down
A voice in the back of my mind
that tells me I don't deserve this

I go back to the ground
because it feels safe
It's not safer
I've just been conditioned
to not believe in myself

Anywho, I Love You

I should have looked at your absence as a gift
Your fingerprints are nowhere in my coding
I wasn't molded under your inconsistent hands
I blamed you for not being invested
I was too young to understand
how I benefited from that
I'm fortunate that your impact was only mild
I get to be who I am, unaltered
by your inability to be a role model

Samantha King Holmes

The night was cold and long
rain cascading down the car window
in a blanket of disgust

Warmth was gone
There were no blankets to cower under
from our harsh reality
There was little heat to spare

Warmth was gone
Not just the kind
to keep your bones from rattling
Warmth had left this family long ago
The kind that makes you trust
that everything will turn out fine

The selfish choices made
that led to this
The denial of responsibility
to other human beings
who now sit in the frigid consequence
of a lack of clear action

Yes, the warmth was gone
The night dragged on
as I watched the droplets climb down the window
I settled into my home for the night
A sad car sitting in the motel parking lot

Anywho, I Love You

It's been ninety days with no conversation
I think we're pretending
that this is lighter than what it is
We've made the decision
to no longer be in each other's lives
I guess our blood isn't that thick
We buried the pain so deep for so long
that we need the world to separate us
There are just things we won't talk about, can't
Someone should have protected us from that
We were always doomed
I'll respect that our lives, for now
don't require the other in it
One day I'll forgive you
Just so you know, writing about this stuff
doesn't make me sad anymore

Let's talk about the people we love
sometimes being the same ones who hold us back
They anchor us in this version of ourselves
that they are comfortable with
Who we're becoming is too much to reconcile with
They prefer we don't aim too high
because aiming small is safer

I'm sorry they didn't protect you
I'm sorry you were only treated like a gift
when someone was taking
I'm sorry the "love" you were given
was really someone else's perversion
I'm sorry you were treated like an object
and not a person

I'm sorry you saw no one as a guide through
the danger you unintentionally walked through
I'm sorry you felt you had to walk through it anyway, alone
I'm sorry for the hard lessons you endured at a young age
I'm sorry you were ever in a position
where you felt the need to disassociate yourself to get through it

I'm sorry for what it did to you
I'm sorry you were pushed to the brink
I'm sorry I didn't stop you from running from it all
I'm sorry I didn't tell you it wasn't your fault
I'm sorry this isn't enough
I'm going to make it right
or at the very least do my best trying to

I didn't realize how much I was lost
in a world of my own making
I'm still there
in that space
biting words eating away
at my self-esteem
pieces of myself scattered
I haven't been able to fix it
I've tried for years
It was already too decimated
Fragments too small for me to put back together
So, I bloom only to wither
Cave back into that space
I've stopped counting the time I spend here
The walls have no more room for the markings
I can't remember a point when it wasn't like this
I'm just having a real hard time
trying to get me to love me

Anywho, I Love You

I shrink into myself
when I don't feel loved
It is too much of a mouthful
to say, "I'm hurt"
It's bittersweet
the things you learn about yourself
through other people

Samantha King Holmes

People are always going to have their opinions
You don't have to adopt them
or weave their doubt into your self-esteem
It is better to have tried
versus deciding not to act
because someone projected
their lack of belief onto you

Anywho, I Love You

I retreated to a quiet place
to get closer to God
I felt that if there were anywhere
He would be, it would be there
and in finding Him
He could maybe
help me find my way back

I've been trying to reconnect to
the person I was before
I allowed myself to be ruined
She was sure of herself
before the world dug its way in
and implanted something different

Here's to the love you gave your all to
only to find that it has made you more cautious
more acutely aware of this world
and how it can get you to accept lies as truth

Here's to the love that has made you stronger
more compassionate toward others
and that has stirred a longing to hold tight to something that lasts

Here's to all the things you called love
that weren't really it

Here's to you for not giving up on yourself
or that powerful feeling inside
that is telling you it's still out there for you
I hope you find it

Lovers took their turns
placing her in a box
They clung to her
She was a flame they yearned to be consumed by
They tore into her
convinced that she held all the answers
A way to happiness

They churned her into a mere craving
No one ever used the word "love"
The intimacy they sought was fleeting
All it took was one person to recognize in her
what she already saw in herself
She won't ever trade meaning everything to him
with being nothing to you

Anywho, I Love You

I remember being there
being so low that I just stayed
I lost sleep, lost my mind
I even lost a larger part of myself
I could sit here and say
"I don't get why you stay," but I do
What I want to say instead
is that you don't have to
Better being out there isn't a myth

This all feels so empty
I think I need a break
I've been living in the world too long
I have its prints on me
I'm starting to carry baggage
that's not even mine
My phone has been in my hand too long
This blue light is awakening all the wrong things
Give me mental stimulation without the burnout
I need a recharge

I adore you at 4am
Don't get me wrong
I love you all day
4am is just a sweet spot
When you're quiet, resting peacefully
Your all too often congested streets lie deserted
No excessive car horns or the sound of drilling in the distance
You're always evolving, never quite complete
Restless energy subsides at this hour
This is the intermission
before you are overrun by ambitious feet
and the relentless drive people have
to prove themselves to you
For now, though, it's just us
and the rare few who prefer your tranquility over your roar

I search for the words to define you
None do you any justice
How can I capture the giant that is your energy?
The depths of your selflessness
Raised by a single mother
so few know the roots of your pain
or the vastness of your perception
I've embarked on a quest to know all your layers
Leaving my loving mark on every scar
I am not perfect; sometimes my words fall short
but it is my mission to make sure
the only words that get tangled with your legacy
are those befitting your passion and devotion
To love you so intensely
that the only story that matters
is the one we've created
And when you look back
you only allow fondness to dance across your mind

On the days when my words are sour
you lean into grace

In the moments when I am cold, aloof
you lean into understanding

The times when I am not my best
you lean into compassion

You always lean in, not away
Steadfast in your commitment
you always lean in, toward me

Anywho, I Love You

Love on me like it's your calling
to make sure I feel it in this life and the next
Accept me whole
without reservation
without alteration
I know this may seem like a lot to ask
but if I am to give you all of me
for a lifetime
I need to know you're all in

You gazed at me
as if captivated
by what God's hands created
Elated, I sat with no words
to bear my feelings
I hope my presence
brings some form of solace

Oh, love of my life
let me be your peace
Let my heart be your home
Allow my soul to feed you
Let my mind bring you stimulation
as my hands tell a story
that my lips won't utter

My body will house our secrets
only for you; it's all for you
I may not be able to convey
it all with words
Share with me this lifetime
I'll show you

RF

LE SUEUR

My toes in the sand
trying not to sink
waves crashing in the background
We laughed so much that day, smiled so hard
It was just us
That was truer to us than anything else would have been
My hair kept getting in my face
There was a fly that kept coming around
We were overdressed for the weather
It was all so wonderful

I've never had to try to fit
You are every place I want to exist
You've always been mine

Find me in every lifetime
I can't bear the thought of loving you just once
I'll be on that beach, sitting under the tree
You know where I mean
I will always look for you
Darling, please look for me

I've tried not to think of any endings
They all take me away from you

You say you're tired
I tell you to wait, as if we have a choice

You are a freedom
I've only ever dreamed of
I took the leap
cause you were standing next to me

Peaceful, you've grounded me
Bold, you've made me fearless

So, let's not speak of endings
I don't think I can bear it
The essence of us
will live within the black, off-white
and the smell of aging pages

Anywho, I Love You

I love the way the early morning sun
creeps onto the buildings and becomes a new skin
How at dusk the clouds
become like cotton candy
The scent of my husband's cologne that lingers in the air
The way his hair feels between my fingers
The face he makes and that little sigh of exasperation
when I stare at him too long
It's like an old song that I know by heart

Right now, I'm thinking about
when we strolled down 42nd hand in hand
Shake Shack, Baked by Melissa, and snacks in the other
We watched a movie and stuffed our faces
That was the first time we had met in person
That was such a good time
The city so new to our love
Now here we are, husband and wife
sitting shoulder to shoulder on the bathroom floor
waiting anxiously in silence
I've already jumped ten steps ahead in my mind, daydreaming
possible names, first word, first steps
Who would you look like?
Who would you cling to more?
If you would pick up our spirit for adventure
or prefer the solace of your own company
In my mind, you already exist
even though we're not sure
Listen, even if you're not here yet
and are out in the universe waiting
I just want you to know that we already love you
Ok, it's time, the two mins are up

Stretching, growing
an evolution happening here
right inside my body
watching it unfold
enduring the aches and the sleepless nights
talking to a soul I hope can hear me
and feel my love through the vibration
It's amazing; it's terrifying
It's the most important job
I will ever have in life

Anywho, I Love You

I didn't know I could be this strong
Twenty-seven hours of my body making way for you
Deep breaths, lots of deep breaths
and hand-holding
A pep talk in my mind
that reminds me the pain isn't stronger than me
The more it comes, the closer I am to meeting you
It was just before 3am when I first heard you cry
I don't remember the pain now
Just getting to hold you for the first time

Anywho, I Love You

My baby lay there, soft and pale
with his father keeping watch over him
He cried out in a shrill for me to come to him

The doctor, nurse, and my doula
like brokers, excitedly put in their bids for my time
regaling over my strength
the immediacy of the delivery
informing me of the cord
that was wrapped around his neck three times
As I silently urged my baby to turn pink, he did

I called out to him
the room fell silent
He knew in that moment
that he was mine
as I am his

Your big, beautiful brown eyes
Those clever little fingers
that reach for everything
I live for your smile and
the dimples that come with it

The fullness of your laughter
The happiness that emanates
from you and fills the room
Any and every time you call out "Mama"
especially when you need me

The way you mimic your father
You, covering our faces in drool-soaked kisses
You, splashing in the tub
Our nighttime snuggles

You are the single greatest collaboration
I have ever been a part of
There are countless things I love about you
my sweet baby boy
Most of all, I am honored
you chose me to be your mother

It's after 5am; our little one
has crawled over to wake you up
I love this part of the day
seeing you two snuggle each other
the joy that's written on your faces

You sweep him up in your arms
head out, and start your day
whispering affirmations in his ear
building him up even before he
understands the importance of words

He is so much like you already
determined, loving, and at times shy
He is your shadow, constantly watching, learning
You give him your all
showing him that there is strength in the soft
affectionate way that you love him

You are the giant whose shoulders he sits on now
and will stand on when he's older
to see the vastness of his potential
and all that you gave
to allow him the chance to dream freely

For now, you both stare at skyscrapers
and the seagulls that fly past our living room windows
There is nothing small about this moment

Son light

Each morning
you come out in search of me
sleepy eyed, arms outstretched
waiting to be held
Love, always so much love
We embrace
this very well being
the calmest moment of the day
We stay there awhile, present
One more little squeeze
before the chaos of the day ensues
Whatever I don't get to in the morning
however it may begin
this is my constant
that you will find me
and start your day
wrapped in my arms

Anywho, I Love You

In those moments
when you fight sleep
I remember
that one day you won't need me to rock you
There will come a time
when you won't feel the need to turn to me
and place your little hand on my face to get rest

It breaks my heart a little to think of this
Time is playing a cruel trick
by having you age so fast
I will always be your security, your safe place
even when you get older
and no longer need
to seek refuge in my arms

You have now been outside my body
longer than you were in it
It still feels like we just brought you home
I know you won't slow down
and that time won't pause for a second
just so I can breathe you in a little more
no matter how much I may want it to

Thank you for being the first to teach us
about this special kind of love
Our home is filled with your laughter, your smile
and your endless energy
Happy birthday, my Sweet Baby Boy
Mommy and Daddy love you immensely

Only two feet tall
you're already a giant
Men would be astonished
if they understood the wisdom you hold
No desire for worldly possessions
just music, playtime, and Momma's affection
I think adults forgot
what it was like to bask in sunshine
and stare into the infinite
You live in moments
You don't have to be trained to
I'll teach you how to master this world
before I ever let it try to sire you
You are a dream brought to fruition
Don't ever let anyone
tell you anything different

I need something for me
To say it out loud sounds ignoble
an ungracious expression
The guilt feels enormous, suffocating, detrimental
It's keeping me from checking in honestly
I ignore it
My breakdowns are hidden, gut-wrenching
and the only release

Anywho, I Love You

I've been feeling off lately
looking outside of myself for the answer
anything to shift me out of this gray space
I'm currently inhabiting
There has been nothing
Nothing has made it better
Nothing has given me guidance to a solution
I still feel empty
I'm still searching

Anywho, I Love You

You miss it
this life growing inside you
After all the aches, nausea
and everything that comes along with it
you are left alone in your own body
only to desire to feel otherworldly again
divine, full

I am trying to capture this moment
to find the perfect words
to contain this jubilation
wrap up all the emotions I feel
I can't find anything that fits
I am excited for your arrival
One day I will get to meet you
Maybe I'll have the words then
I don't think I will
or that I will need them
My sweet little one

Her little hand wrapped around your finger
Big brown eyes curiously searching yours
A moment of recognition
when she hears your voice for the first time

Her first smile at you
The boo-boos you will kiss
and the nightmares you'll chase away
Her taking ownership of your nook

I look forward to watching your bond grow
Her learning the meaning of love
by how you treat her

I can continue to list
all the things I can't wait to see
but most of all it's the love
that she'll learn about
from your devotion to our family

She's growing each day
I can't wait for you to meet
I hope she has your calm reassurance
and a bit of my bravery

Her little limbs exploring my insides
gliding seamlessly, curiously
I feel her growing stronger
ever more impatient
She, unaware that's she's waiting
oblivious to what the next chapter holds
I'm ecstatic for her debut
and to watch her shape her world

You are love
and the greatest person
I will ever be
is because you made me that
I will pour into you
with all I have

I will nurture your confidence
so that the thought that
you are not enough
doesn't ever creep into the back of your mind

If there is anything I could give you
an abundance of in this life
it would be happiness

Moonlight

If you catch even a glimpse of daybreak
making its way across the sky
you are wide awake
looking at me
searching for the sun
I am engulfed in your smiles
and high-pitched laughter
I rush from the living room
into the office for fear
that our little household will erupt
just from hearing your joy
You are soul rich
the purest form of love

Maybe this is heaven
these little fingers that are on my neck
the rise and fall of his chest
this peace before he wakes up
and tosses everything around the apartment

Perhaps heaven is really my daughter's smile
and how she loves me without question
the way her eyes light up when she hears me sing
that face she makes when she wants kisses
her hand wrapped around my thumb as she goes to sleep

What if this is heaven?
and we're all just waiting
for an absolution we already reside in?

Currents of change
streaming down my frame
evidence that I housed two beings
The ripples they've created
are felt so much further than just my body

I hear his feet pounding
on the floor
as he runs
her gurgles a steady accompaniment
in the background

I know this so well now
Their routines, my schedule
Their growth, my devotion

I housed two souls
Now here they are
these manifestations of love
personalities shaping
minds expanding
light beams who have yet to learn
their own power

To the little girl in me

I hope you like the life
I've created for us
We've done so many of the things
we used to dream of

Our words have made it across the world
Our deepest thoughts and feelings
now rest peacefully in so many hands
We made it to Venice
We've explored Rome
We feel in love with Paris

Manhattan is home
Central Park our backyard
We have walked all over this city
capturing its beauty as we see it

We have our own little family
two kids and a husband
that you love dearly
This place is whole and sacred
I, you, we protect it

You are safe here
You don't have to search
for your place
in the world anymore

Kit mains libres recommandé.
CET AFFICHAGE
JCDecaux
CAFE BORDS DE SEINE
CAFE
RESTAURA

Anywho, I Love You

I stand here
washing the dishes
watching the soap swirl along
the edge of the plate
The water seeping into my skin
creating this temporary view
into a future where they will be weathered and old

These two hands
that gripped so tightly to my panda bear
Picked honeysuckle from the backyard
for the perfume I wanted to create
That picked grapes off the vine
in Grandpa's backyard

These small, powerful giants
that fought the boys back
That one over the other climbed trees
and caught me when I fell out

These lovely, graceful purveyors
of my most cherished thoughts
rushing across pages
Trying to keep up
with the spill pouring from my mind

These hands that sweat profusely when nervous
found their match
They held on tightly throughout
every adventure across the globe
They walked down an aisle gripping onto forever

Purposefully, gently, and with the greatest of love
they lifted my son
held him to my chest
caught my daughter
when she was born
covered in promises and devotion
Now they tickle them throughout the day
and cradle them during bedtime

These hands know all the stories
Have endured and felt the pain and joy
Now here they are, covered in suds
happily washing away
the remnants of today's meals
youthful and wise

Just when you think
you have it all figured out
talk less and listen more
Everything you know now
compares nothing with what you could still learn
When you get offended, check your defenses
Work on resolving the triggers before deciding to react
Negative words won't ever get to touch your light
if you don't let them
People have issues they haven't quite acknowledged
Don't take on their problems
They aren't yours to bear

Andrews McMeel Publishing
a division of Andrews McMeel Universal
1130 Walnut Street, Kansas City, Missouri 64106

www.andrewsmcmeel.com

22 23 24 25 26 RR2 10 9 8 7 6 5 4 3 2 1

ISBN: 978-1-5248-7805-4

Library of Congress Control Number: 2022938924

Editor: Patty Rice
Art Director/Designer: Diane Marsh
Production Editor: Elizabeth A. Garcia
Production Manager: Julie Skalla

ATTENTION: SCHOOLS AND BUSINESSES
Andrews McMeel books are available at quantity discounts with bulk purchase for educational, business, or sales promotional use. For information, please e-mail the Andrews McMeel Publishing Special Sales Department: sales@amuniversal.com.